Original title:
A Handbag of Hope

Copyright © 2025 Creative Arts Management OÜ
All rights reserved.

Author: Aidan Marlowe
ISBN HARDBACK: 978-1-80586-065-5
ISBN PAPERBACK: 978-1-80586-537-7

A Pocketful of Light

In my bag there hides a spark,
A little joy, a cheeky lark.
With a wink and playful grin,
I chase the gloom, let laughter in.

A crumpled note, a fortune found,
A silly hat, oh what a sound!
I toss in smiles, a sprinkle of cheer,
It's a party when I'm near!

Dreams Unfolding in Leather

Beneath the flap, my wishes sway,
They dance and twirl, come out to play.
A candy bar and an old receipt,
A ticket stub that feels so sweet.

Each pocket whispers tales of glee,
Of dreams that wander, wild and free.
With every zip, a new delight,
My leather dreams take off in flight.

The Embrace of Adventure

In shadows deep, I stash my maps,
A dash of humor, and silly scraps.
With every pull, adventures tease,
Unfolding laughter with such ease.

A compass spin, I chase the sun,
In peculiar places, oh what fun!
Each twist and turn, a giggling twist,
Adventure calls, how could I resist?

Whispers of Resilience

In fabric folds, the stories cling,
Whispers of hope, like birds on wing.
A broken crayon, a worn-out shoe,
Reminders that I made it through.

With every clash and merry call,
My spirit rises, won't let me fall.
These little treasures, quirks so bright,
Keep me standing, day and night.

Unraveled Threads

In the depths of my purse, a sight so absurd,
Candy wrappers dance, like a flock of birds.
Broken dreams nestle, along with loose change,
Each crumpled ticket hints at something strange.

Lipstick half-melted, a vibrant pink tease,
Forgotten receipts serve as my memories' keys.
A mysterious sock, a lint-covered snack,
I find treasure in chaos, there's no looking back.

The Carrier of Kindred Spirits

Within this pocket, friendships reside,
Caramel whispers and laughter collide.
Old gum wrappers, where secrets conspire,
Echoes of giggles, like vines they entwire.

A tiny umbrella for sunshine's surprise,
Came out to play, but forgot its disguise.
Socks paired with sandals, in the most daring way,
Fashion advice? Well, I'll live for today!

Reflections of Resurgence

A mirror reflects a face, oh so spry,
But inside my bag, it's a carnival nearby.
Snacks on parade, my hunger they curb,
A wild goose chase for that lost little verb.

A comb with a history, quite tangled indeed,
Whispers of laughter, the soul's deepest creed.
With each quirky item, I find a new tale,
In this jumbled fusion, I set forth to sail.

The Joy Within the Strain

Oh, the weight of my bag, a burden, you say?
It's a treasure chest where my worries can play.
A dance of old tissues, bits of confetti,
Each twist and each turn makes my spirit so ready.

A wallet of wonders, where dreams can take flight,
Stamped with the stories that shimmer so bright.
Though clutter may reign, it's a heart full of cheer,
For within all this mess, joy manages to steer.

Stitched Together in Faith

A zipper that's stuck, oh what's the fuss?
Pockets full of dreams, they chase the bus.
Lint and loose change, life's little mess,
Yet in this wild bag, we find our success.

Flaps of ambition, patterns of cheer,
Carried by laughter, nothing to fear.
A crumpled old map, adventures in store,
We'll stitch each moment, then add a few more.

Hidden Light

At the bottom lies glitter, a dazzling find,
A forgotten sandwich, just keep it in mind.
Beneath the chaos, a spark may ignite,
In this cluttered realm, shines a whimsical light.

The keys to the world, they jingle and jive,
Amidst all the nonsense, we barely survive.
But with laughter in hand and a wink at the night,
Hidden treasures emerge, oh what a delight!

The Clasp of Confidence

A twist and a turn, the clasp gives a cheer,
Daring our worries to disappear.
With each little snap, we gather our quirk,
In this stylish embrace, we find how to work.

The mirror reflects all our wildest schemes,
As we strut through the world, chasing out dreams.
With a wink and a grin, let the fun never stop,
For confidence holds us, right up to the top.

Boundless Aspirations

Overflowing with wishes, this bag never closes,
With wild little hopes and a sprinkle of roses.
A ticket to laughter, a compass to cheer,
We travel through life, with opinions sincere.

Bouncing on clouds, with giggles and grace,
In this jolly old bag, there's always a space.
So pack up your joy, no limits in sight,
Boundless together, we dance into the night.

Carried Dreams

In a purse so bright and bold,
Lie dreams much bigger than gold.
With glitter, sparkles, and a grin,
It whispers tales of where we've been.

A snack for now, a toy for later,
And always room for a paper skater.
A mirror acts as my best friend,
Reflecting hopes that never end.

Echoes of Grace

Amidst the clutter, find a shoe,
It's mismatched, but what's it to you?
A ticket stub, a gum wrapper,
Each tells stories, a joyful chapper.

The keys to laughter, a lip balm bright,
Even a spoon for a midnight bite.
Here's the charm, we can't ignore,
With every find, I love it more!

The Weight of Wishes

Inside this bag, odd things collide,
A rubber duck, where secrets hide.
A fortune cookie, slightly stale,
Whispers stories we should unveil.

A glitter pen, my writer's tool,
And candy wrappers—oh, the fool!
Each wish is packed in layers thick,
In laughter and fun, we find our trick.

Beneath the Fabric of Tomorrow

Underneath, hopes dance in thread,
Like little fairies, they're well-fed.
A twinkling charm, a scrap of lace,
All dreams fit snug in this small space.

With a poke and a prod, I dive right in,
Pulling out smiles, one by one, as twin.
Tomorrow calls, let's not delay,
With whimsy packed, we'll laugh and play.

Pages of Possibility

In my bag, there's a tiny cat,
A rubber chicken, and a little hat.
A kazoo that sings, a mirror that glows,
And crumbs from snacks that nobody knows.

A ticket stub from a show gone wrong,
A fortune cookie, where I don't belong.
A bottle of giggles spilled just right,
And a glittery star that shines so bright.

Each pocket hides a secret surprise,
With dancing socks that twirl and rise.
A spoon for soup, a fork for fun,
And a magic wand that can't be undone.

So when I reach in for some delight,
I find the joy wrapped up tight.
For in this jolly, quirky sack,
There's laughter waiting, I won't hold back!

The Canvas of Now

Inside this pouch, I'm quite the artist,
With crayons, paint, and a cupcake that's the hardest.
An empty jar for wishes I've made,
And a pair of shoes that dance unafraid.

Sketches of dreams on napkins and wraps,
Jokey postcards, and silly snaps.
My paintbrush swirls with flavors and sights,
Like pizza slices spun in the lights.

There's glitter to sprinkle on everything near,
And socks that tickle with laughter and cheer.
A canvas to capture the joy of today,
With doodles that giggle and dance in the fray.

So let's color our afternoons bright,
With goofy creations that feel just right.
In this magical space of whimsy and fun,
Every moment's a masterpiece before it's done!

The Hidden Map

Under layers, a map with no bounds,
Leading to laughter and silly sounds.
It whispers of treasures, both big and small,
Like jellybeans hiding behind a wall.

Curves and twists, it's a puzzler's delight,
To find where the giggles are hidden in sight.
A dragon that snores under beds full of dreams,
Chasing rainbows through candy streams.

With an X that marks the spot of a game,
And the laughter of friends calling my name.
A detour to whimsies, a shortcut to cheer,
With a compass that only points to good cheer.

So follow the lines, let the journey unfold,
With stories of wonder and silliness told.
For items aplenty, all tucked away tight,
Lead us to happiness bright as the night!

Threads of Tranquility

In this funny pouch of peace and cheer,
A jigsaw puzzle and a rubber ear.
With threads that giggle and colors that hum,
And plush little pillows where giggles come from.

A cozy blanket to snuggle up warm,
For silly storms that bring no harm.
Yarn balls of joy tangled in knots,
And socks that dance on whimsical spots.

Each patch tells a tale of laughter and sighs,
With quirky faces and wide-open eyes.
A tapestry woven with snickers and fun,
That twirls and fluffs in the sun.

So let's stitch together our silly days,
With these threads of joy in whimsical ways.
In this lovely scatter, we find our bliss,
For a laughter-filled life is a wonderful twist!

Mosaic of Memories

In a purse of whimsical tales,
Beneath the snacks and broken scales,
Lies a map of mishaps and cheer,
Each crumpled note, a heartfelt leer.

A lipstick's wander, a gum's embrace,
Forgotten receipts, a jumbled space,
The keys I've lost, the ones I've found,
Dance like confetti on the ground.

A tiny mirror reflects my dreams,
With laughs and wishes in funny schemes,
A locket holding giggles like halls,
Nestled in pockets, a treasure that calls.

In this jolly mix, the chaos sings,
Adventures wrapped in random flings,
Life's little joys in a frayed old threads,
A colorful patch where friendship spreads.

Fluttering Fragments of Dreams

Inside a bag of vibrant flair,
Chasing wishes that dance in air,
Napkins holding secrets and hope,
Fumbling laughter, a tightrope.

A rubber duck can brighten my day,
With a wink and a quack in a quirky way,
A crumpled wish list, oddly outdone,
By a slice of pizza and a sprinkle of fun.

Fading receipts tell stories untold,
Of ice cream spills and moments bold,
In pockets of joy, I feel so spry,
Collecting giggles 'neath a clear blue sky.

So here's to the fragments that flutter around,
In the haven where my dreams are found,
Each trivial piece, a laugh on this ride,
An eclectic treasure, my heart open wide.

Icons of Inner Strength

With buttons and bling tucked all around,
A quirky charm in treasures found,
Each keychain tangled in laughter's chime,
Proving I'm brave, one whimsy at a time.

A paperclip holds bits of my glee,
While the chocolate wrapper whispers to me,
The world in my bag, a carnival scene,
Where laughter and chaos make life routine.

Polaroids catch moments, wild and wacky,
Dance like a dervish, never too tacky,
With glittery smiles and stories that burst,
In crumbs of cookies, I'll quench my thirst.

So here's to the icons of what I believe,
That in life's parade, I've much to achieve,
Wrapped up in joy, every whimsy embraced,
A treasure trove of memories interlaced.

Wandering Souls and Wanderlust

In this vessel of laughter, I roam,
Collecting oddities, far from home,
With a travel tag that's seen better days,
Its adventures coated in quirky ways.

A fortune cookie's message, crumpled and torn,
Reminds me of journeys in the early morn,
Each shimmy and shake while I strut around,
Sparks joy in my bag where hopes are found.

With mismatched socks as my fashion crown,
I stroll through life with a chuckle, not a frown,
The essence of wanderlust blazes bright,
In doodles and doodads, dancing with light.

So here's to the wonders inside my delight,
The mischief and mirth that makes it just right,
A traveler's heart in a tapestry spun,
In this bag of treasures, life's a wild run.

Grains of Grit

In my bag, I keep a snack,
A crumbly cookie, sweet and cracked.
A dash of grit, a pinch of zest,
Life's little bites, a tasty quest.

With every crumb, a tale I weave,
Of silly days when I believe.
Laughter echoes, as I munch,
Finding joy in every crunch.

A dusty old book, a silly pen,
Little treasures from way back when.
Each grain of grit, a joy unbound,
In the chaos, silliness found.

So come along, bring your own cheer,
With crumbs and giggles, let's persevere.
In our bags, we carry light,
Ready for a laugh, day or night.

Sails of Serenity

In my purse, a tiny sail,
It flaps and flutters, a funny tale.
Of breezy dreams and sunny days,
With every gust, it sways and plays.

A rubber duck, a little charm,
It quacks and giggles, brings no harm.
The winds of smiles fill the air,
As I navigate without a care.

Each wave of laughter, a fresh embrace,
Time to unwind, a soft-paced race.
Balloons of joy, they float and fly,
Sailing smoothly through the sky.

So grab your sails, let's set a course,
For fun and laughter, we're a driving force.
With each new breeze, we'll dance and glide,
In seas of joy, with hearts open wide.

Tides of Renewal

When life feels heavy, like a stone,
In my quirky bag, I find my tone.
Shells of laughter, waves of glee,
Each tide brings quirks that set me free.

A pair of socks, mismatched in style,
These little quirks make me smile.
Each tide of laughter washes ashore,
With every wave, I ask for more.

Sandcastles built with dreams and cheer,
A bucket of giggles, my troubles disappear.
Renewal comes with each ocean toss,
I collect the waves, count not the loss.

So let us surf on hope-filled seas,
With tides of renewal, we catch the breeze.
In every splash, an echo's found,
Together we laugh, ring the joy around.

Hope on the Go

In my bag, a map tucked tight,
Drawing paths to pure delight.
With each twist, a giggle grows,
Adventures whispered, as hope flows.

A rubber band, a silly fling,
It snaps with joy, oh, what a thing!
As I bounce along the street,
Every hop feels light and sweet.

A silly hat, bright and bold,
Wearing dreams worth more than gold.
With every step, I dance through time,
Finding puns that softly rhyme.

So come along, let's wander wide,
With hope in hand, joy as our guide.
In all the places we will go,
We'll find the funny, let love glow.

Cadence of Care

In the depths, a snack lies tight,
Munchies saved for a midnight bite.
Lip balm dancing, so sleek and bright,
Concealing worries, a jovial sight.

With a mirror reflecting my grin,
I practice my charm, let the fun begin.
Keys that jingle, a cheerful din,
In this treasure trove, I always win.

A tiny umbrella, a burst of glee,
For rain or shine, it shelters me.
Among the odds and ends, you see,
I conjure laughter and jubilee.

So here I stand, bag in tow,
Carrying secrets, both high and low.
With every trinket, there's room to grow,
A whimsical world, I'll gladly stow.

In the Stitch of Time

A needle here, a button there,
Fixing life with crafty flair.
Threads of laughter everywhere,
In my patchwork purse, I declare!

Chaos inside, yet it's all just fine,
Searching for chapstick, I find a pine.
Stitched with stories that intertwine,
Each pocket a memory, a quirky line.

Old receipts tell tales of fun,
Dancing at dusk until we're done.
With every mess, we've surely won,
Explorations wrapped in a pun.

So here I am, with laughter galore,
Finding joy in the mundane store.
With whimsical stitches, I do much more,
Crafting hope from the fabric of yore.

Brushstrokes of Belief

Colors splashed in a spacious pouch,
Paints of laughter, here I crouch.
Creativity whispers, never a slouch,
In this vibrant dream, I gladly vouch.

Brushes dancing, twirling about,
Inspiration's canvas, never in doubt.
With every stroke, a joyful shout,
Artistry lived, without a drought.

Silly sketches, a flower or two,
Memories crafted, in bright hue.
Carried with love, my heart's debut,
A whimsical world in colors true.

So let's create in this joyful spree,
With laughter as paint, we're wild and free.
Every idea, like honey from a bee,
Shaped with belief in our creativity.

Carrying Light

In my satchel, a giggle blooms,
Light as a feather, escaping glooms.
With each trinket, joy resumes,
Like sunshine bursting through the rooms.

A flashlight glimmers with playful grin,
Illuminating paths, let the fun begin.
With whimsical sparks, we draw folks in,
Carrying banter, where have you been?

Jokes tucked deep in hidden seams,
Life's little treasures, like sweet dreams.
In laughter's embrace, everything gleams,
Together we float on friendship's beams.

So join this ride, let your spirit soar,
With every moment, we're seeking more.
In our collective light, we will explore,
Wrapping the world in laughter's core.

Pearls of Wisdom

In a bag with gleaming lights,
I found a slice of cake at night.
Wisdom, it seems, has a sweet side,
With crumbs of laughter that I can't hide.

Each trinket holds a tale or two,
Like socks that vanish, who knew?
A mirror with a quirky wink,
Reminds me not to overthink!

A secret stash of goofy charms,
To keep away the stress alarms.
With every jingle, joy will bloom,
It's light and bright, not filled with gloom.

The Weight of Goodness

There's a feather in my purse so light,
But inside, it feels just right.
Each good deed adds a little weight,
Walking wobbly, but ain't that great?

I might trip or dance around,
With kindness in my pocket found.
A snack for sharing, what a treat,
A way to turn strangers to meet!

Giggles spill from every seam,
Goodness wrapped in a quirky dream.
Still I ponder, 'Is this too much?'
Then I grin and give a touch!

Canvas of Connection

A color splash in every fold,
Stored laughter and stories untold.
Oh, look! A paintbrush, how divine,
To doodle dreams and sip on wine.

Friendship paints with vibrant hues,
Laughing at our silly shoes.
In this space, all shine and glow,
Creating bonds, just like a show.

With every squiggle, joy will sprout,
Connecting hearts, no doubt, no doubt!
Let's keep our canvas filled with cheer,
As we sip soda and play the deer!

Beneath the Surface

Dive deep into pockets unseen,
Whispers of giggles, what a scene!
A rubber duck, an old receipt,
Who knew my purse held such a treat?

Beneath the layers, treasures hide,
Lost keys and doodles taking a ride.
A compass broken, but still bright,
Leading laughter into the night.

Every item has a funny tale,
With memories set to sail.
So open up those hidden doors,
And let the smiles and chuckles soar!

The Journey of Little Things

In pockets deep and bags so wide,
Small treasures hide, no need to bide.
A lost sock peeks, a snack-sized treat,
Oh, what a life, it's quite the feat!

A lipstick tube, with colors bright,
Promising glam, nearly takes flight.
A rogue penny, worth not a dime,
Yet somehow feels like a perfect rhyme.

Some crumpled notes, bits of old dreams,
A rubber duck that loudly screams.
Each little thing has its own tale,
Adventures lived beyond the pale.

So here's to those little, strange finds,
Each one unique, our hearts it binds.
With laughter and glee, we pack with care,
Our journey continues, let's fly through air!

Lap of Tranquility

In a cozy nook, my bag does rest,
A plushy toy claims the very best.
Lip balm whispers, 'Pamper that pout!'
While the cat just watches, all curled out.

Bottles of giggles and jars of dreams,
Underneath, there's a world of themes.
A napkin crumple sings a soft tune,
As I sip my tea, under the moon.

A compass lost, yet never adrift,
Navigating joy, what a perfect gift!
Each pocket's a puzzle, quirky and bright,
In the lap of calm, everything feels right.

So here's to the odd, the bizarre and sweet,
Every little item, a kindred treat.
With laughter and lightness, let's cherish our space,
In this curious purse, life's peculiar grace!

Hues of Happiness

In my pouch of sunshine, just take a peek,
A rainbow speckled sock and a glittery cheek.
A crayon scribble, a doodle that sings,
Every bit scattered, joy gently clings.

Tiny trinkets, laughing in glee,
A pencil with hopes of a grand marquee.
Forgotten receipts tell stories anew,
When dancing with friends, and splashing in blue.

Bubbles in bottles, full of delight,
Bright marbles waiting to roll in the light.
Each object a treasure, a memory's spark,
Filling our hearts till we're lost in the park.

So here's to the oddities, bright and true,
In every small thing, there's nothing we rue.
With laughter painting the world all around,
Hues of happiness, joyfully found!

Carried with Grace

With style and flair, I strut the lane,
Email reminders all swim in my brain.
A sticky note offers me wise advice,
'Hold on to laughter, and nothing's a vice.'

A brush here, a pen there, such a display,
An odd mix of treasures, guiding my way.
All things I cherish, but none quite defined,
As I dance through life, leaving worries behind.

Tissues, like petals, finely arranged,
Wipe away frowns, all feelings exchanged.
A whistle of joy, it rings through the beat,
For grace isn't just, but all about heat.

So let us embrace the chaos within,
Life's wild adventure is where we begin.
Carried with laughter, and quirks on display,
Every little moment, a bright, sunny day!

Stitched with Courage

In pockets deep, we find our dreams,
With zippers that squeak, or so it seems.
Adventure awaits in every seam,
With a sprinkle of laughter, we'll make a team.

Among receipts and a half-eaten snack,
Lies courage wrapped in a stylish pack.
Each thread a tale, a quirky little quack,
Stitched together, ready to attack.

Fuzzy keychains jingle with glee,
Reminders of joy, wild and free.
With a wink and a nod, we hear the decree,
Life's a grand show, let's sip that tea!

So rummage around, what do you see?
A world of wonders, oh let it be!
With pockets of laughter, come share with me,
Who knows what treasures await in jubilee!

A Clutch of Aspirations

In a tiny clutch, we hide our dreams,
Sprinkling glitter, or so it seems.
With each little wish, our laughter beams,
Life's a funny play, full of funny themes.

A tangle of lip gloss, a rogue old gum,
Each quirky item, oh isn't it fun?
We juggle our hopes, just like a nun,
Spinning through life, like we're on the run.

Hope peeks out, from a pocket so sly,
Waving its hand, saying, "Oh me, oh my!"
A sprinkle of joy, wings ready to fly,
Let's giggle and dance, give it a try!

So clutch your dreams, don't let them fade,
Twirl through the chaos, don't be afraid.
With laughter and cheer, the world is made,
In this funny journey, let's all cascade.

Tucked Away Treasures

In the depths of the bag, wonders reside,
Chocolate wrappers, a price tag that lied.
The quirkiest bits, where secrets abide,
With each little find, our hearts open wide.

Old pens that don't write, a comb full of fluff,
Memories hidden, both silly and tough.
A pinch of nostalgia to gobble up stuff,
Life's full of treasures, and some just rough.

Like mismatched socks, our dreams intertwine,
Dancing through chaos, sipping on wine.
In pockets of laughter, we brightly shine,
Who knew life could taste so divine?

So let's dig deep, with giggles we'll play,
Unearthing the treasures that brighten the day.
In a world full of quirks, come join the ballet,
For joy is the treasure tucked away!

Glimmers in the Dark

When night falls low, and giggles ignite,
Look inside your bag, find hope's shining light.
With keychains that twinkle, all snug and tight,
Our dreams dance around, what a silly sight!

A stray snack crumbles, a chocolatey trail,
As we rummage and search, we happily sail.
In pockets of joy, we set our own sail,
Traveling the paths where laughter won't fail.

With stickers and doodles, our hearts take flight,
In this whimsical ride, we embrace the night.
Gathering sparkles, our spirits feel bright,
Oh, how the world glimmers in delight!

So here's to the treasures tucked safe and snug,
With laughter and joy, the universe we tug.
In corners and shadows, we joyfully shrug,
For inside our bags, we're eternally snug!

Sheltered in Dreams

In the depths of my purse, oh what a sight,
A kaleidoscope of wonders, shining bright.
Lipsticks and chapsticks, oh, so divine,
Keys to adventures, all perfectly aligned.

Candy wrappers whisper secrets untold,
Memories of laughter and stories unfold.
A crumpled receipt from lunch long ago,
Reminds me of joy in the ebb and the flow.

A tiny old mirror reflects all my schemes,
While pockets of wishes cradle my dreams.
In this funky abode, I twirl and I spin,
Finding gems in the chaos, let the fun begin!

So here's to the quirks that life has to give,
In this whimsical pouch, I learn how to live.
Each treasure I clutch is a giggle, a glee,
For hope is the laughter that sets my heart free!

Phantoms of Past Possibilities

Beneath the flap, specters dance with delight,
Voices of choices whispering 'not quite'.
Old tickets and trinkets, they cheerfully chime,
Echoes of dreams, all frozen in time.

What ifs like balloons float, colliding with fate,
Dancing the cha-cha, oh, isn't it great?
A watch without minutes, just ticks in a trance,
Turns burdens to jest in a whimsical dance.

A rogue bit of fluff springs to life with a grin,
Sparks of my past, let the comedy spin.
Flip through the pages of laughter and tears,
Each shadow a friend through my whimsical years.

So I'll welcome these phantoms, these characters bold,
Jesters of time with their stories retold.
For hope wears a mask made of giggles and glee,
Bringing forth joy from what used to be.

Tokens of Tomorrow

From the depths of my bag, I pull out a dream,
A fortune cookie slip, a whimsical scheme.
Noodle-swirled visions, so wild and so wide,
Possibilities bloom like flowers inside.

A marble that twinkled, a promise of play,
Rolling along in the light of the day.
With every quick glance, I hoot and I holler,
For hope's a grand bank where the happy hearts pour.

A notebook half empty, with doodles so bright,
Scripted in crayon, my future in sight.
Chapters unwritten wait, eager to fly,
While laughter bubbles up, reaching for the sky.

The tokens of tomorrow, they giggle and wink,
Encouraging whimsy, they never let me sink.
For in this mad moment, I find all I need,
Hope wrapped in joy, a hilarious seed!

Radiating Resilience

Amidst the chaos, I thrive and I glow,
With sparkles of laughter, outshining the woe.
There's a glittery pen tucked snug in my pack,
Scribbles of hope, there's no turning back.

Bubbles of humor, they rise and they pop,
In this circus of life, I'm a comedic top.
Fuzzy socks wait for cozy-mood nights,
Giggles of warmth to win all the fights.

Throw in a cocktail of dreams and delight,
A sprinkle of kindness, keep spirits in flight.
Though storms may roll in, I'll still find the jest,
With laughter my anchor, I'll pass every test.

So here's to resilience, my quirky little muse,
With hope as my compass, I've nothing to lose.
In my playful satchel, adventures await,
For joy is my armor; let the fun celebrate!

Unseen Emotions

Inside this pouch, a snack or two,
A mirror for a quick 'ooh-la-la' view!
Lipstick smiles that hide the doubt,
Who knew such joy could come about?

Forgotten fortunes and old receipts,
Dancing dreams in crumpled sheets.
A lost pen sings a silly tune,
Spilling secrets to a tired moon.

Each jingle tells a tale so sweet,
Of quirky trips and strangers' feet.
Emotional snacks tape up the seams,
Silly treasures cradle our dreams.

In pockets deep, we stash absurdity,
A cozy nook of absurdity.
With laughter tossed like confetti fine,
We carry joy in this tiny shrine.

Shimmering Hopes

A glittery keychain swings with grace,
Hopes embrace in a silly space.
Bobby pins and gum wrappers unite,
Creating a vision all shiny and bright.

A phone that rarely rings but glows,
In this neon purse, possibility grows.
Socks without matches, where do they go?
Each lonely item come put on a show.

Coins tumble into a dazzling dance,
As dreams spin round for a second chance.
Underneath scattered wishes' flight,
Hope gives a wink in the fading light.

With laughter that ripples through what's been,
A bubbly spirit flows within.
A sparkly trinket, a glimpse of cheer,
Shimmering joys that soon draw near.

The Embrace of Kindness

A hello sticker for friends so dear,
Wrapped in smiles ready to share.
A napkin with doodles of quirky glee,
Kindness fits snugly in this spree.

There's a toy dinosaur, bright and small,
Bringing laughter, reminding us all.
A homemade card, a heartfelt note,
In the rhythm of giving, kindness floats.

A cozy caboodle of heartfelt bits,
Fashioned from laughter and silly fits.
This purse holds hugs with a raucous cheer,
Wrapped in a giggle, it's all sincere.

Every zipper opens a tale of fun,
A sprinkle of kindness for everyone.
With the jingling of coins, hearts ignite,
In this embrace, mischief shines bright.

Tapestry of the Mundane

In this chaotic weave, life does strut,
A bunch of crumbs and a sharp little cut.
Socks that danced their way to the fray,
Are stories of laughter gently at play.

An old receipt with pizza dreams,
Collecting sunshine in silly beams.
A bottle cap of favorite soda,
Makes the boring moments become a fiesta!

Lip balm whispers sweet escape,
As keys jingle, in a merry shape.
This patchwork holds neurosis-based glee,
A twirl of the mundane turns topsy-turvy.

Bright snippets shine through each crease,
In the fabric of life, oddities release.
With quirky treasure, we laugh and float,
In this whimsical tapestry, we gloat.

Secrets in the Stitching

In seams where laughter hides,
A tiny bird chirps, then glides.
With pockets deep, and zippers bright,
It holds my dreams, both day and night.

A button whispers silly tales,
Of socks and keys, and chocolate trails.
Each fold contains a quirk or two,
Adventures waiting, just for you.

Oh, what a caper, this colorful sack!
It dares me to keep things on track.
With every purse, a new surprise,
A giggle bursts and laughter flies.

So take my hand, let's roam in glee,
Together our secrets, just you and me.
In every stitch, a joy we'll find,
A crafty wonder, oh so kind!

Threads of Possibility

In the weave, a strand of cheer,
A twist of fate can appear near.
With every pull, a giggle grows,
As luck unfolds in funny prose.

Oh, this fabric of the wildest dreams,
Hides silly toys with squeaky screams.
Each thread unfolds a tale to tell,
Of minor mishaps, oh so swell!

The yarn of chance, it spins and twirls,
In here, the oddest fates unfurl.
With every tug, an awkward dance,
As hope transcends in a quirky chance!

So let's unravel each knotted thought,
With laughter stitched, and joy well-wrought.
In pockets deep, let whimsy flow,
With threads of fun, we reap and sow!

The Purse of Possibilities

In the depths of this quirky bag,
A pickle jar and a rubber tag.
With whimsy packed, it knows no bounds,
As giggles hide in silly sounds.

A fortune cookie, half eaten yet,
Promises of laughter, you won't regret.
What treasure lies in this jumbled spree?
A whoopee cushion? Yes! Count me!

Each clasp a door to fun unknown,
A mishmash of things, and none outgrown.
With every opening, joy is found,
As smiles erupt, and laughter's sound!

So let's embark, just you and I,
With curiosities stacked up high.
Tap into this vibrant stash,
Unlock the giggles in a flash!

Cherished Tokens of Tomorrow

With trinkets stashed and charms galore,
Inside this pouch there's always more.
A rubber duck and a tiny shoe,
What curious joys will we pursue?

A giggly key from some faraway land,
Unlocks the laughter, so well-planned.
A memento from a fumble or fall,
Each token whispers the best of all.

Oh, let's collect these gleeful finds,
As tomorrow's mischief unbinds.
With every smile, the world expands,
In our little pouch, joy forever stands!

So, take a leap, embrace the jest,
Each cherished token is simply the best.
With every trinket, let laughter reign,
As the road to joy we'll gladly gain!

The Joyride of Life

Life's a bumpy ride, just hold on tight,
Laughs and giggles in the fading light.
With snacks and dreams all packed away,
We'll roll through troubles, come what may.

Turn up the tunes, let the laughter soar,
With quirky friends, who could ask for more?
Every twist and turn a new surprise,
With glittering joy in our sparkling eyes.

Bumps in the road? Just a chance to dance,
In this wild trip, we'll take a chance.
Confetti storms and rubber chicken fights,
Oh, how these moments feel just right!

So here's to us, the wacky crew,
On life's joyride, there's plenty to do.
With whimsy in heart and laughter in store,
Let's crank the fun to a hundred and more!

Embracing the Journey

With each step we take, there's joy to be found,
In puddles of laughter upon the ground.
So pack up your quirks, don't leave them behind,
Embrace every moment, be silly, be kind.

Lost in the woods? Let's build a grand fort,
With twigs and old socks, we'll never fall short!
We'll go on adventures with wild, crazy dreams,
And sip on our woes with ice cream extremes.

The world's our playground, with swings made of cheer,
We'll ride on the seesaws, casting away fear.
With polka dot maps and a treasure to seek,
Life's all about laughter, not just the peak!

So hold on to fun, let worries take flight,
With friends by your side, everything's bright.
Dance through the journey, with giggles in place,
Life's a grand fiesta, let's join the race!

Beneath the Fabric

Tucked in the seams, there's magic galore,
With laughter and wishes, and giggles in store.
Each pocket a treasure, a whimsical find,
A sprinkle of joy, to lighten the mind.

Beneath the surface, where secrets are spun,
Stories of mishaps, oh what silly fun!
With glittering threads, we'll stitch our own lore,
Creating a tapestry to endlessly explore.

A button of brilliance, a patch made of glee,
Colorful tales, just waiting for thee.
Unfold every wrinkle, let laughter burst free,
Together, we'll weave the oddest marquee!

So here's to the fabric that life has bestowed,
With each stitch and fold, let the fun erode.
In the quilt of our dreams, let's snuggle and play,
Creating our stories in the silliest way!

The Keeper of Secrets

Inside this little box, laughter held tight,
With secrets and giggles, it's pure delight.
A sprinkle of chaos, a dash of surprise,
In the keeper's embrace, oh how time flies!

Whispers of joy like bubbles in air,
With tales of the silly, we've plenty to share.
As we zip and we zoom 'neath the whimsical hat,
The keeper just chuckles at this and that.

From socks with odd patterns to dreams of the night,
The secrets we hold make everything right.
In this playful space, we dance and we cheer,
With a wink and a grin, we keep fun near.

So let's lift the lid, let the laughter unfold,
With secrets unspun, worth more than gold.
In this little treasure, where humor resides,
We'll find endless joy as a friendship abides!

Lasting Impressions

In the depths of my purse, a wild adventure,
Lipstick and crayons, a strange mixture.
Who knew my handbag could double as art?
With each grab for a pen, a creative start!

Forgotten receipts in a chaotic pile,
A ticket for a concert from two years a while.
It's not just a bag, it's a time capsule,
Each trinket inside tells a tale quite ample.

Worn-out gum wrappers and fluff everywhere,
My bag's like a jungle filled with strange hare.
You need a snack? Just reach and explore,
You might find a granola that's gone on a tour!

Next time you peek into that bulky abyss,
Remember, it holds the world's quirkiest bliss.
With each jangle and rustle, a laugh will arise,
For what's in a handbag? Just endless surprise!

Trinkets of Tomorrow

A deck of old cards, a fortune-teller's treasure,
Each draw from my bag brings a pinch of sheer pleasure.
Chasing the future with laughter and glee,
In this whimsical pouch, what will there be?

A keychain shaped like a tiny pinecone,
What stories they've seen, what dreams they've known!
Time flies with trinkets filled with delight,
From scratch-off tickets to glitter so bright.

A sewing kit whispering, 'Just one quick stitch,'
When fashion emergencies cause dreams to glitch.
Ode to a button, so noble, so round,
A fashionista's prayer where remnants are found!

So here's to the treasures we fondly collect,
A laugh in each pocket, what else would you expect?
With every foray into this whimsical vault,
Tomorrow's fun nestled in chaos and jolt!

The Elegance of Endurance

In my vintage bag, there's a tale of the past,
Each scuff and each scratch, memories amassed.
They say fashion fades, but I beg to differ,
With each pop of color, my spirit will quiver.

A mirror that's cracked, a reflection of me,
Who knew vanity thrived in less symmetry?
Yet each glance takes me back to sweet days,
When elegance rocked in the silliest ways.

Lip gloss that's ancient yet smells like spring,
Oh, how it clings to my hopes like a string!
With a swirl and a swipe, I'm a queen on the scene,
In a bag filled with giggles and dreams bright and keen.

So here's to the charm that never goes out,
A purse full of joy, that's what it's about.
With a wink and a grin, we endure with flair,
Timeless and funny, a fashionable pair!

Journey Within the Closure

As I zip up my bag, a world of surprise,
A snack, a spare sock, and crumbled wise lies.
Each closure's a promise, a secret untold,
What's nestled in velvet, we'll surely behold!

A key ring that jingles with tales of the wild,
An umbrella so small, but courageous it smiled.
When raindrops collide, it's there to defend,
My journey's best ally, my colorful friend!

And what of the pens, a rainbow of hues?
They dance on the page with whimsical muse.
Each clog of the tip tells a story anew,
In the journey ahead, I'll pen something true!

So here's to the zippers that hold all we fear,
A bag full of laughter, no need to adhere.
With each twist and turn, let adventures unroll,
For it's not just closure, it's joy for the soul!

Dreams in the Lining

In the depths where secrets hide,
A candy wrapper takes a ride.
Loose change jangles with delight,
A treasure trove, oh what a sight!

Forgotten ticket from a show,
A slip of paper, 'Win a Joe!'
With giggles caught in silly threads,
Each little find unfolds the heads.

Button lost from old blue jeans,
The residue of coffee beans.
A mint that's past its prime, it's true,
But still, it's like a gumdrop view.

So chase those dreams within your bag,
Embrace the quirks, don't start to lag.
For in the lining's joyful maze,
Are hints of laughter, oddly phrased.

The Secret Compartment of Light

Beneath the flap, where shadows play,
Lies a realm where socks can sway.
A flashlight hides, but not from me,
It sparkles like a mystery!

With every zip, there's joy anew,
A rubber duck just quacked, it's true!
A bottle cap from summer's past,
Each whimsy holds a tale vast.

Maybe notes from friends or foes,
Accompanied by giggles, who knows?
A tiny mirror reflects my grin,
A memory drawn from where I've been.

So open up that secret space,
And celebrate its joyful grace.
For light may shine from oddest places,
Bringing smiles to all our faces.

Purseful of Possibilities

With every clasp, there's chance and cheer,
A moment's wish can magically appear.
A concert ticket from a month gone by,
Brings back the fun, oh me, oh my!

Doodles scrawled on napkins wide,
A treasure map where hopes reside.
A keychain from a friend's abode,
Can lead you down a giggle road.

With strings of yarn and crumbs galore,
This purse holds laughter and much more.
A fortune cookie's fate awaits,
Wrapped in laughter that never abates.

Embrace the odds of what's inside,
With every find, let giggles slide.
For life's a jest in joyful loops,
In every purse, the magic stoops.

Echoes of the Heart

In the depths of fabric dreams,
A whisper laughs in playful beams.
A lost earring with tales to spin,
Echoes of moments, let's dive in!

Notes from kids with silly rhymes,
Witty phrases, timeless chimes.
A tiny doll that strikes a pose,
Each trinket tells where laughter grows.

From snack wrappers to broken pens,
Every item sparks some amends.
A wrinkled map, a sweet surprise,
Turns mundane trips to joyous highs.

So cherish echoes and let them sing,
A symphony from quirky bling.
For in each cranny, a heartbeat starts,
A joyous dance of hidden arts.

Embers of Inspiration

From the pockets, dreams do sprout,
A crumpled list, no doubt!
With gum and glitter in the mix,
Who knew hope was in the fix?

Wand of mascara, a pen that won't write,
A snack for courage, just out of sight.
Photos of friends, the silly ones too,
Oh, what magic these bits can do!

A mirror shines back, who's that? Oh wait,
A vision of laughter, it's never too late.
With sequins and sparkles, we dance through the fray,
Each item a treasure, come join the ballet!

So let's dig deep, explore the fun,
In this cheerful chaos, we've already won.
With whimsy and giggles, let's surely cope,
For inside this bundle, lies all our hope!

The Keeper of Dreams

Inside this satchel, fabric and thread,
A thousand daydreams from a sleepy head.
With a rubber duck and a tiny toy car,
Who needs a fortune? We're already a star!

Tangled headphones, beckoning song,
Notes of optimism when things feel wrong.
A crayon, a napkin, to sketch out a fate,
Just doodle your worries, it's never too late!

Silly stickers of rainbows and cats,
To brighten the moments when life's in spats.
An eraser for error, a pencil for fun,
In this treasure chest, we've only begun!

So let's celebrate whims, let's gather the zest,
For every odd item becomes our best guest.
With laughter our anchor, we'll sail through the night,
Together we'll dream, oh, what a delight!

Symbols of Strength

In my trusty pouch, there's plenty of flair,
A bottle of glitter, a breath of fresh air.
With each little trinket, my spirit will rise,
Who says all heroes wear capes in disguise?

A spool of bright thread, for stitching my fears,
Patterns of joy woven through the years.
With a pinch of confetti and a dash of delight,
We can conquer the world, or at least avoid fright!

A "Get Out of Jail" card with pizza on it,
When life gets too serious, I give it a hit.
Pens of all colors to write down my schemes,
My roadmap to laughter and whimsical dreams!

So, gather your treasures, let's dance in the light,
With friendship and fun, we'll shine oh-so-bright!
In this playful arsenal, we'll find our way,
With symbols of strength, we'll seize the day!

Beneath the Veil of Uncertainty

Ha! What's that lurking? A mystery check,
A mix of oddities, a kooky wreck.
A sock with a smile, a spoon that can dance,
Life's little surprises—a curious chance!

A note from a friend, "Keep calm and have tea,"
Wrapped in a napkin, a moment for me.
With rubber bands, joy is stretching its legs,
Who knew hope is nestled with all of these pegs?

A fuzzy old keychain, tales of old fights,
In the depths of my carry-all, they spark quirky nights.
A flashlight for giggles when darkness descends,
Together we'll twinkle, oh, how laughter transcends!

So here's to the whimsy, the joy in the sway,
Let's embrace uncertainty, come what may.
With each little oddity, we'll shake up the night,
For in playful chaos, we find pure delight!

Enveloped in Sunshine

With pockets of laughter, I skip down the street,
Waving at trouble, can't be beat.
My satchel's a treasure, full of bright cheer,
It glows with the sparkle of things I hold dear.

Sunshine's my buddy, we dance all around,
Even my shoes have begun to astound.
I carry my dreams in a quirky old sack,
Facing each day with a giggle and quack.

There's a snack for the journey, oh what a find!
A smudge of jelly that bubbles my mind.
Nothing too heavy, just joy in a pouch,
Chasing the clouds, giving doubt a good couch.

So here's to the moments, both silly and bright,
With giggles and glitter, I take on the night.
When life throws some shade, I just give it a wink,
For in this strange handbag, I'll never sink!

Crumbs of Courage

Biscuit bits trail in my bag with flair,
Each crumb a reminder, life's sweet and rare.
When worries come knocking, I offer them crumbs,
A nibble of bravery, my heart softly hums.

With cupcakes of giggles and sprinkles of fun,
I strut through the chaos, away I run.
If challenges rise, I just flick out a snack,
With frosting on top, I won't hold back!

Each morsel of courage, a light on the way,
I munch on my dreams and brighten my day.
A mix of bizarre and moments so grand,
I dare to believe, with snacks on my hand.

So here's to the nibbles that give me my edge,
Crumb by small crumb, I jump off the ledge.
With laughter and buttercream filling my soul,
I'm off to conquer, for I am whole!

The Veil of Serenity

Wrapped up in giggles, I float like a cloud,
In my whimsical purse, I stand tall and proud.
With a charm that's contagious, I wave bye to dread,
Each pocket a prayer, a wish deftly said.

When troubles encircle, I pull out a grin,
A tiny blue elephant, he squeaks with a spin.
"Don't worry!" he shouts, "we'll dance through the mess!
Just twirl with delight, and the world will bless!"

With whispers of peace and a tap of my neat,
I'm giggling away, life's silly elite.
Confetti of kindness fills up my small share,
In this quirky delight, I find comfort and flare.

So let's skip through the madness, with joy as our guide,
With a wink and a chuckle, the chaos can slide.
For wrapped in my laughter, I'll face any fright,
In sweet, silly moments, I steal the limelight!

A Vivid Collection

In the depths of my bag, a world full of dreams,
Each trinket a story, bursting at seams.
A rainbow of whimsy, it dances with flair,
Each piece holds a giggle, light as the air.

There's a hat with a feather, bright pink and absurd,
With a wink and a nudge, it speaks without word.
And a squeaky old toy, just a tad out of tune,
Whispers secrets under the bright, silly moon.

With jars full of sunshine and giggles galore,
I may take a leap, or just waltz to the shore.
With a sprinkled confetti, I'll brighten the way,
My vivid collection will savagely play!

So bring on the laughter, let's twist and let twirl,
With stories that shimmer, we'll flourish and whirl.
For in my dear purse lies a vast, silly sea,
Of joy and of courage, just waiting for me!

Journey in a Zipper

In a bag with a zipper, my treasures all gleam,
A half-eaten muffin, and a lizard's old dream.
Keys that won't unlock, lip balm from last fall,
Each item a story, come one, come all!

I reach for my wallet, find a sock instead,
A neon pink one where my money once led.
Laughter erupts when I share my sweet finds,
In this journey of zippers, absurdity binds!

With each silly object, I chuckle and grin,
A rubber ducky, oh where do I begin?
The joys of the unexpected, a comic delight,
In the depths of my handbag, there's humor in sight!

So here's to the wonders that jingle and dance,
It's a wild little ride, not a mere circumstance!
For within every pocket, each fold holds a tease,
Adventure awaits, if you just give a squeeze!

Holders of Light

My bag is a beacon, with colors so bright,
It draws in the giggles, and chases away plight.
With pens that explode, like a comedy scene,
I'm armed for the laughs, always ready and keen!

Inside dwells a stash of old candy and dreams,
Wrappers of glory, oh how sweet it all seems!
I pull out a gadget, not sure what it's for,
The holders of light, they keep me wanting more!

Out pops a shiny star, a keychain encore,
Each trinket I gather brings joy to the core.
I'll whip out a clown nose, or a silly old hat,
And soon, we're all laughing, where there once was a spat!

So I carry this treasure, it sparkles, it shines,
With laughter as armor, we'll reveal life's designs.
My handbag is magic, a pouch full of cheer,
Bringing light to the shadows, we've nothing to fear!

Folds of Fortitude

Like origami dreams hidden well in a clutch,
Folds of the fearless, they give laughter a touch.
A crumpled-up napkin boasts life advice true,
Fold it, unfold it, and find joy anew!

There's a pencil for sketching a world with a grin,
With doodles of joy wrapped snugly within.
A bottle cap charm, it jingles with glee,
These folds of fortitude, they carry me free!

In the corners I find half-forgotten delights,
A joke on a slip, how to tickle the nights.
So I gather these pieces, like puzzle, they fit,
With each wacky fold, life's laughter is lit!

So remember, dear friend, what this bag can bestow,
Folds of fortitude, with a cheeky hello!
Embrace all the quirks that your journey unveils,
In the heart of your handbag, it's laughter that sails!

A Pocketful of Positivity

With a pocketful of giggles, I step out the door,
A feather from laughter, who could ask for more?
Holding bubbles of joy that twist and then pop,
Each burst is a chuckle, I just cannot stop!

From marshmallow smiles to forget-me-not dreams,
I carry a world bursting at its seams.
A fortune cookie slip, 'you'll laugh with delight,'
Brightening my travels, way into the night!

So I dig through my treasures, my little great finds,
There's glitter, there's silliness, joy intertwined.
In every pocket, positivity blooms,
Chasing all shadows, dispersing the glooms!

Let us share in this journey, where laughter entwines,
A pocketful of joy, both yours and mine shines!
So gather up giggles, let's spread them around,
In the pockets of life, true happiness found!

Embracing the Unexpected

In a bag of wonders, I sometimes find,
A half-eaten cookie, quite unrefined.
Lipstick that's missing, a broken pen,
But laughter erupts, again and again.

Old receipts whisper tales of delight,
Like the time I thought late-night snacks were right.
A squashed-up napkin, a ticket for fun,
Every odd treasure shines like the sun.

When life throws curves, I rummage around,
Hope's hidden gems in my mishaps abound.
This chaos I carry makes living a ride,
With pockets of laughter, joy's my guide.

Embrace the weirdness, let smiles take flight,
In every odd corner, my heart's feeling light.
Unexpected treasures? Bring them on, please!
In a bag full of joy, my spirit's at ease.

Soft Pockets of Joy

A candy wrapper crinkles, a little surprise,
A ticklish sensation, the giggles arise.
Crushed dreams of mints, oh where did they go?
I chuckle and sigh, as I put on a show.

Stickers and trinkets from places unknown,
Flashbacks of laughter, memories grown.
Fuzzy little creatures sneak in when I roam,
What's this? A teddy? I'll call it my home.

There's fluff from a snack, a crumb from a joke,
In this pouch of delight, life's a weird cloak.
The softest of pockets hold giggles and glee,
Wrapped in weird treasures, just silly old me.

Each pull of a whim, a laugh on display,
A sprinkle of joy, brightening my day.
So here's to the soft, the silly, the bright,
In my whimsical world, everything feels right.

Fabric of Faith

Torn edges and frays, with threads intertwine,
Stitching up laughter, let's sip on some wine.
Grandma's old quilt holds tales of the past,
In every stitch, a memory cast.

Colors collide like a dance on a spree,
Each patch a reminder of who we can be.
Faith holds us together, like fabric in seams,
Through laughter and chaos, we weave our dreams.

Duct tape and yarn fix most of our woes,
Who knew that calamity leads us to prose?
A seamstress of moments, I stitch and I patch,
With needles of joy, life's chaos I hatch.

So let's wear this fabric, rejoice and parade,
In the quirky design, our friendships are laid.
Faith in the silly, and love in the winks,
In this tapestry, hope forever blinks.

Keys to the Future

I've got keys galore, they jingle and sing,
Unlocking tomorrow, oh what fun they bring!
A rainbow of shapes, some rusty and bent,
Each opens a door, where giggles are sent.

A key to my schedule, a key just for snacks,
Unlocking adventures, oh, what a whack!
Turn, twist, and wiggle, let's see what's in store,
In this silly treasure, there's always much more.

A key to my heart, a key to my dreams,
In the toolbox of friendship, joy always beams.
With laughter as fuel, we spark up the night,
The keys to the future? They shine ever bright!

So let's jingle and jive, with each turn of a key,
Building our pathways, so happy and free.
Here's to the laughter, the chances we take,
With keys in our hands, the world's ours to make.

A Container of Imprints

In the depths of a purse so wide,
A cat's old toy is tucked inside.
Forgotten snacks sing tales of cheer,
And odd receipts yearn to disappear.

Lipstick's gone rogue, it marks a trail,
While crumpled gum holds secrets pale.
A coin from July, a key to nowhere,
What treasures hide in this fashion fair?

Unmatched gloves play hide and seek,
While shopping lists make a fashion critique.
An old sock whispers, 'I was a pair!'
What magic hides, do we even dare?

Through chaos and clutter, we shuffle along,
Each item a verse in a silly song.
With laughter and whimsy, we find our way,
In this whimsical world, we joyfully sway.

Dreams in Delicate Canvas

A canvas bag with paint all smeared,
Holds dreams of travels, or so it's presumed.
Strawberries squished, it's clichéd, I know,
Yet every splatter inspires a show.

Inside are notes from oddball friends,
And crumpled maps that never quite end.
Art supplies mingle, chaos on parade,
With each swirl of color, new stories made.

A tangle of chargers in vibrant hues,
Sings the blues of outdated tech news.
Lip balm whispering, 'I've got your back,'
While receipt rolls pile up in a stack.

In this fragile pouch where memories blend,
Life's messy sketches become our best friend.
With laughter we scoop up each crumpled piece,
A delicate canvas, the chaos won't cease.

Unfolding Grace

From depths of fabric where dreams reside,
A bouncy ball in the corner doth hide.
With ribbons and paperclips tangled round,
The elegance here is totally profound.

An old umbrella, with stories of rain,
Whispers of sunshine, washing out pain.
Hopes like marbles, they scatter and roll,
In this grand adventure, we find our whole.

A glitter pen scrawls goofy delight,
Jokes written sideways, things light as a kite.
With tea-stained pages, wisdom drips slow,
Doodles of joy, on the heart's canvas flow.

Through mishaps and laughter, we dance with grace,
In this unfolding, we find our place.
Embracing the chaos, it fuels our fire,
For in every stumble, we reach even higher.

The Spirit Inside

In a quirky pouch where laughter's stored,
Lies a spirit bright, never ignored.
A comb that's lost its teeth, oh dear,
Yet for untamed hair, it's still quite near.

A mismatched pair of glasses hides,
With sparkling lenses, where humor resides.
Old gum wrappers, like memories, cling,
The laughter they brought is an endless spring.

Within dull pockets, the jokes take flight,
A sharp pencil poised, ready to write.
With rubber bands rattling, fun's just begun,
This vibrant spirit dances like the sun.

So let's dive deep in this whimsical chest,
Where silliness reigns, and laughter's a guest.
With every odd item, we smile with pride,
For in this container, joy cannot hide.

The Hidden Oasis

In a bag so small, treasures abound,
A snack, a book, lost cats to be found.
Lipstick and gum, a mirror to smile,
A spoon for the soup? Well, wait just a while!

It holds a tiny world, all crammed and tight,
A sock for the cold and a flashlight for night.
Old tickets and coins, a map with no name,
It's like a magician's hat, quite the wild game!

Inside, it's a jungle of oddities rare,
A rubber duck ready to take on the dare.
Forgotten notes, some old gum, a toy,
Finding little gems? Oh, what a joy!

In this chaotic space, life's wonders unfold,
Each item a story, a memory retold.
A surprising escape from the mundane grind,
With each little find, a new laugh we find.

Whispering Wishes

Deep in the depths, secrets collide,
A spoon, a napkin, a tiny slide.
Dreams tucked away, just waiting to pop,
Like confetti in winter – oh, what a hop!

The keys to the kingdom, oh what a chore,
Found a candy wrapper and a high-heeled shoe score!
A dance with a lollipop, twirls in the air,
Each wallet-sized wish, floating everywhere.

An umbrella for spring, and glitter galore,
Why do I have bubble wrap? I'm not sure!
With silly finds, like a toy army man,
Ready to conquer my snack – that's the plan!

Every twist and turn, new laughter I hear,
A mystery bag, like a treasure, my dear.
Whispers of joy in the folds and the seams,
It's a giggle machine, bursting at the seams!

Curves of Comfort

A pouch so round, curves wiggle with glee,
A warmth in my heart, as I rummage with glee.
In search of a snack, a soft comfy sock,
It's like a soft pillow, an odd little rock!

Once a wild ride, a dance of delight,
Now there's a sock monkey caught in the light.
An ancient receipt? Oh, what can it say?
Maybe I bought happiness that fateful day!

A squishy chapstick, all flavors to taste,
Nibbles and giggles, zero time to waste.
The curves of this comfort pack stories so neat,
With laughter unfolding, each pocket a treat!

From spices to paperclips, all piled together,
Who knew such treasures could bring such fun weather?
With a twist and a twirl, I hold it up high,
A wonderland waiting, come on, let's fly!

A Sprinkle of Stardust

Fluffy and sparkly, it glitters and beams,
A bag full of laughter, it dances with dreams.
Crayons and glitter, a cupcake stamp fair,
Each whimsy-wrapped tale whispers stories to share.

A magic-wand pen, it twirls and it spins,
With wisdom from kittens and strength from the winds.
A wild little dance, pulls at my heart,
With each silly treasure, I'm back at the start!

Old buttons, a collar, a fortune-cookie slip,
Each element sings, gives my spirit a trip.
Stardust behind me, I wander and sway,
With every sweet charm, the gray skies give way.

A sprinkle of joy, like rainbows in jars,
Each pocket's a galaxy, full of bright stars.
An adventure awaits in this magical space,
A sprinkle of laughter fills up every place.

A Cloak of Positivity

In a world of knots and strings,
I wear my joy like a silly hat.
Each day brings laughter's flings,
And I juggle dreams like a circus brat.

Inside my cloak, there's a dancing shoe,
With polka dots and a vibrant hue.
I twirl and spin, oh what a view,
As sunshine bounces where worries flew.

A laugh, a sigh, they often collide,
But I skip through puddles, full of pride.
With a wink at clouds, I take the ride,
And wear my smile like a festive tide.

Each pocket holds a quirky surprise,
A whoopee cushion, a joke to advise.
In this merry mantle, I rise,
Finding joy in life's goofy ties.

The Guardian of Dreams

Oh, a pillow of wishes sits on my shelf,
Guarding hopes while I laugh at myself.
With a feathered quill, I scribble a plan,
To wake up a giant, a very small man.

In the corner, a calendar grins,
With cat pictures and misplaced pins.
I'll tick off each day with a dance and a spin,
As each silly mishap turns into wins.

Magic socks and mismatched shoes,
They help me choose when there's nothing to lose.
With gummy bears and a joke that ensues,
Every crazy thought I gladly peruse.

With glittering stars that giggle and shine,
I hop on the train of the fun-loving line.
Chasing moonbeams, oh, so divine,
For in dreamland, my mischief aligns.

Whispers of Resilience

A picnic basket, broken yet bold,
Holds cookies crumbling, tales retold.
With each crumb, a giggle escapes,
In the dance of life, we wear silly capes.

Beneath the table, the dog steals a fry,
While we toast to the moments that slip on by.
We squeak with laughter, oh me, oh my,
Turning disasters into a pie in the sky.

With a sprinkle of chaos, I start to hum,
Finding joy in the jittery drum.
For the whispers of hope say, "Here we come!"
As we bounce back, ready to overcome.

In the pockets of fabric and in dreams subtly sown,
We uncover the laughter that's always our own.
With each resilient beat, brightly grown,
Life's a party we've happily thrown.

Threads of Tomorrow

With yarn of laughter, I weave the day,
Knitting plans in a quirky display.
Each stitch a giggle, each knot a cheer,
I craft my future, with nibbles of beer.

Socks with stripes that clash in delight,
Turn into stories by day and by night.
With a croissant jammed in my pocket tight,
I march on the path that feels just right.

In the laughter of looms that dance in a row,
I find the colors of dreams in a flow.
With a sprinkle of magic, they start to glow,
We're stitching a fabric where hope gets to grow.

While sewing my visions, I riotously smile,
For every thread is worth every while.
In the quilt of tomorrow, I'll wrap up my style,
And leave trails of joy wandering a mile.

www.ingramcontent.com/pod-product-compliance
Lightning Source LLC
Chambersburg PA
CBHW051730290426
43661CB00122B/212